St. Clare School
12455 Coventry Hills Way NE
Calgary, Alberta

This is a teddy bear. It looks a little like a wild bear and it may have fur somewhat like a wild bear, but hold on! A wild bear has pointed teeth, powerful jaws and sharp claws. A real bear is unpredictable and should not attend tea parties or sleep with you. A wild bear should not be hugged, fed, followed or posed with for photos. What are wild bears really like and how should we treat them?

These are black bears and often they really are black (especially in the East), but what a confusing name for a bear that also comes in shades of brown, blond, cinnamon and even midnight-blue (especially in the West). In parts of Western Canada you can even see black bears that are all white!

Black bears live right across North America wherever the woods provide enough space, shelter, food and water. (Not in cute little cottages or cozy caves with name-plates on the door) Each bear needs a range of about 20 miles (32 km) in all directions. They climb trees like pros to reach fruit and nuts or to escape danger. Just because wild black bears naturally prefer being in the woods and sleeping at night, don't think they won't show up any time and any place food is easily found.

Grizzly bears are usually much bigger than black bears. They have a distinctive hump on their shoulders where black bears don't. Their claws are much longer and better suited for digging than climbing. The digging is what develops their large muscled shoulder hump. Their shaggy splotchy fur can be anywhere from blond to almost black. Pale-tipped guard hairs are longer than the thick mat of fur and give some bears a "frosted" appearance.

As one of the strongest living animals in North America, a grizzly's might is breathtaking. It could harm just about anything it wants to with one powerful swipe of a paw. A mother protecting her cubs can be especially dangerous. She can move across rough ground at 44ft (13.5 meters) per second! Obviously, you want to stay well out of her way, and get this...the feeling is mutual! Grizzlies would almost always rather avoid people if possible. Due to habitat loss and conflict with human activities grizzly bear range and population have declined dramatically in North America. Their homeland has become more isolated and restricted to higher treeless areas, valley bottoms and tundra. The remaining grizzlies live in Western Canada, Alaska, and a few small pockets in Northwestern US. (see map page 17)

Don't let the look of a wild bear fool you. The plodding creature seems to lumber and loaf around, moving its great hulk with effort. That's just the fat and fur disguising a quick and nimble muscular body. In a split second this rambler can turn into a swift predator, charging faster than a race horse can run. Bears also have great endurance, running 10 mi (16 km) without stopping, and swimming 2 mi (3.2 km) at a time.

Bears are distant relatives to dogs, wolves and foxes and like these animals they are curious, intelligent, clever and playful. They learn rapidly, they can reason and they have excellent memories. Bears share some human traits also. They walk flat-footed, have footprints and skeletons similar to ours, and they can stand upright. A bear cub in trouble sounds much like a human baby crying.

Bears are among the best sniffers of all. This very keen sense of smell locates mates, identifies cubs, and detects food. Bears can track down mates or meat several miles away. They have been known to detect a human scent 14 hours after the person has passed by!

It's a good thing bears can smell so well because it helps them find the food they need, and bears need an enormous amount of food. They are so famous for their big appetites that we sometimes hear people declare themselves as hungry as bears. Even the smell of scented cosmetics, chewing gum, and toothpaste can attract a bear. Just look how far away they can smell things! Although bears will eat just about anything, it is best for them to find only foods that occur naturally in their ranges.

When bears first come out of their dens in spring they are groggy, sluggish and thirsty. They may have gone five months or more without eating, drinking or producing waste. If mother bears have new cubs, they are extremely protective of them. The cubs stay with mom about a year and a half while learning how to find food and stay out of trouble.

Bears are the only really large omnivores (they eat both plants and meat), but more than 75% of their diet is just plant products. Until things begin to grow in the spring, bears chew on roots, bark and buds to get protein. A bear is more likely to starve at this time than during the long winter denning period. A bear loses between 20% and 40% of its weight while denning and continues to lose weight until the middle of summer when food is more plentiful. As things start to sprout they graze on grasses, wildflowers and tender new plant shoots and leaves. As the summer progresses their appetites become bigger than ever. They gorge themselves on berries. (One researcher studied a bear that ate 200,000 buffalo berries in one day!) And they devour nuts and acorns too. Just about every waking minute is spent on the pursuit of food.

Bears love honey almost as much as their cartoon characters suggest. They eat the bees, the honey and the whole nest, but the main attraction is the bee larvae. This gain is not without pain. Bears suffer through painful bee stings and swelling for their reward. Older, more experienced bears learn to get the goods with less torment.

Bears can trap fish under their claws in shallow water and snatch them up with quick strong jaws. Grizzly bears do more fishing than black bears. They might toss some fish up on shore so their cubs can practice the art of slapping and trapping the slippery meal. The "white" black bears of British Columbia have been known to dive right under water to get fish. Although adult bears live and travel alone, they will tolerate each other at a fishing hole or berry patch where there is plenty to go around.

Occasionally bears take great pleasure in chasing and snaring a rodent.
They may tear up a large area in happy pursuit of the small meal.
Fish and small mammals account for about 1% of a bear's diet.

Bears tear apart logs and tree stumps and turn over rocks to
find grubs. They eat grasshoppers while grazing and
they'll whack the top off an anthill and lick
up the ants with their long tongues. It may
seem like a tiny
trifling snack, but
every little bug helps fill
up a bear and they can
eat thousands. One bear
being studied ate 25,000
caterpillars in a day!
Bugs and insects make up
5-10% of a bear's diet.

Like any of us, bears like an easy meal. Although grizzly bears may take down a young or weakened hoofed animal, bears are not very capable hunters. Fast-food for them is an animal that has already been killed by something else. These carrion meals make up 10-15% of a bear's diet. Sometimes they stash a carcass, planning to enjoy the leftovers later. (If you find animal remains, leave the area quickly before the rightful owner thinks you've come to share his dinner!)

It may seem that because bears are so able-bodied, so fast, so smart, so strong and so resourceful, their survival is a sure bet. Yet, considering the huge quantity of food they need and the large distances they may need to travel, it is not so simple. Each adult bear needs a territory that provides enough water, food and shelter to survive. Male bears especially need very large territories.

Unfortunately, bears have lost much of their habitat to human activities such as real estate development, farming, ranching, mining, logging, oil and gas development, roads, tourism, recreation, hunting, poaching and off-road all-terrain vehicles. These pressures force bears into areas where they are in direct conflict with humans, areas that don't provide enough food, and areas too isolated for bears to find mates.

Bears find homes in many public lands and parks of all kinds.
These are National Parks where black bears live.

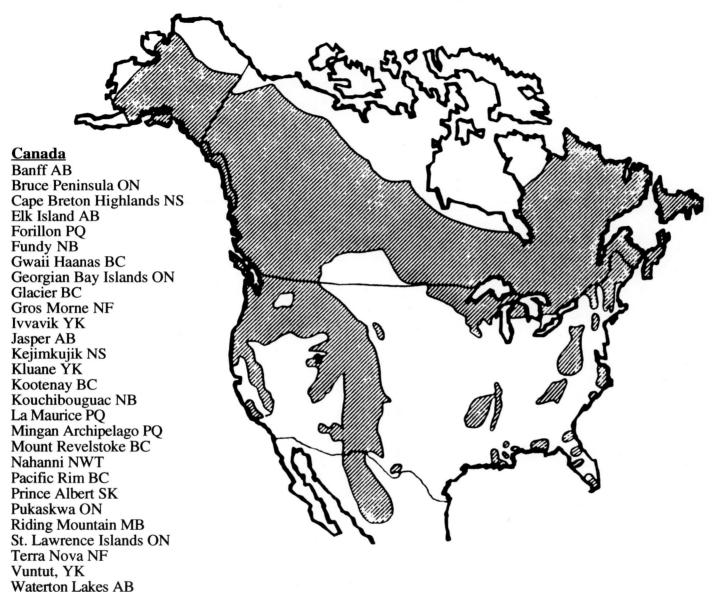

**Canada**
Banff AB
Bruce Peninsula ON
Cape Breton Highlands NS
Elk Island AB
Forillon PQ
Fundy NB
Gwaii Haanas BC
Georgian Bay Islands ON
Glacier BC
Gros Morne NF
Ivvavik YK
Jasper AB
Kejimkujik NS
Kluane YK
Kootenay BC
Kouchibouguac NB
La Maurice PQ
Mingan Archipelago PQ
Mount Revelstoke BC
Nahanni NWT
Pacific Rim BC
Prince Albert SK
Pukaskwa ON
Riding Mountain MB
St. Lawrence Islands ON
Terra Nova NF
Vuntut, YK
Waterton Lakes AB
Wood Buffalo AB, NWT
Yoho BC

**United States**
Acadia ME
Big Bend TX
Bryce Canyon UT
Canyonlands UT
Crater Lake OR
Denali AK
Everglades FL
Gates of the Arctic AK
Glacier MT
Glacier Bay AK
Grand Canyon AZ
Grand Teton WY
Great Smoky Mountains TN
Guadalupe Mountains TX
Kenai Fjords AK
Kobuk Valley AK
Lake Clark AK
Lassen Volcanic CA
Mesa Verde CO
Mount Rainer WA
North Cascades WA
Olympic WA
Redwood CA
Rocky Mountain CO
Sequoia-Kings Canyon CA
Shenandoah VA
Voyageurs MN
Wrangell-St. Elias AK
Yellowstone WY
Yosemite CA

Black bear range map
courtesy of the USFWS

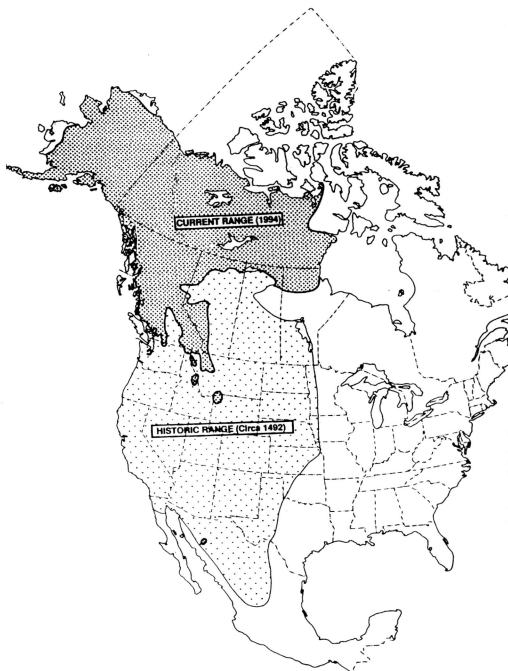

Grizzly bear range map courtesy of British Columbia Ministry of Environment, Lands, and Parks

## Grizzly bears live in these National Parks

### Canada
Banff AB
Glacier BC
Gwaii Haanas BC
Ivvavik YK
Jasper AB
Kluane YK
Kootenay BC
Mount Revelstoke BC
Nahanni NWT
Vuntut YK
Waterton Lakes AB

### United States
Denali AK
Gates of the Arctic AK
Glacier MT
Glacier Bay AK
Grand Teton WY
Katmai AK
Kobuk Valley AK
Lake Clark AK
North Cascades WA
Wrangell-St. Elias AK
Yellowstone WY

The grizzly bear's population and range are less than half of what they were before European settlement. Their numbers are stable in Canada's North Western and Yukon Territories. However, the grizzly bears are losing ground everywhere else they live: Alaska, Idaho, Montana, Washington, Wyoming, Alberta and British Columbia. Thankfully, much research, planning and education is underway to try and keep bears healthy and safe.

Our parks were created to preserve some of the space and natural resources bears need to survive. Since parks are also meant for people who want to enjoy unspoiled space and the wildlife it supports, we have to learn to share it without getting in each other's way. Now it's time to meet the most dangerous animal in the park.

A human who feeds bears, or thoughtlessly leaves food, garbage, cooking equipment or cosmetics where bears can get at them, is the most dangerous animal in the park. Bears who learn to associate people with food become dangerous and doomed.

In the past, before we knew any better, campers and park visitors used to purposely attract bears by feeding them. The tourists would then watch and photograph the bears at close range. Souvenir shops sold postcards depicting traffic lined up and stopped, bears leaning in the car windows or catching doughnuts in the air.

We eventually learned the hard way that these bears become aggressive and lose their natural fear of humans. Bears have caused great damage to people, cars and equipment while in pursuit of chips and marshmallows. They are wild animals and they do not sit up and beg in circus fashion. They break, bust, drag, grab, rip, claw and gnaw their way to whatever smells like food. Many bears have had to be destroyed because people had changed them. Others have been unsuccessfully relocated at great expense. Most relocated bears either returned to the campgrounds or failed to survive in their new territory.

Now we know better. Parks with bear populations hand out information and instructions at their entrances. It's our responsibility to use the bear-proof garbage containers, and to store all food, drinks, dishes and coolers in food lockers. If these are not provided, ask park staff about the best storage methods and precautions to use at your campsite. Never keep food, dishes or cosmetics in your tent. Don't cook near tents or sleeping bags because they absorb cooking odors. Don't cook fresh smelly food. Freeze-dried is best. Eat all that you cook and throw out things with strong odors. Treat anything that has touched food or absorbed its odors as bear bait and store it as you would food. Store cosmetics the same way and don't keep them or snacks in your pockets!

Remember, due to the clever nature of bears, no precaution or storage method is guaranteed. Bears can unscrew jar lids, open door latches and recognize packaging, uniforms and vehicles. Never underestimate a bear!

Bears who have not tasted our food will likely choose to avoid people whenever possible, yet the scent of food or garbage may still attract hungry bears. Different parks use various methods to discourage bears from visiting peopled areas. They include negative reinforcement such as rubber bullets, pepper spray, loud gunshot noise, and specially trained bear-chasing dogs. If a bear persists in returning to peopled areas, park staff may relocate the bear as a last resort. The bear has to be shot with a sleeping dart. While drugged, the animal is examined, measured, tagged, and fitted with a radio collar.

By keeping track of a collared bear, park staff can monitor its behavior and make sure it's staying out of trouble. Relocation of campground junkies is used less and less because of the high cost and low success. If a bear continues to be a nuisance and a threat to humans, it has to be killed before it hurts someone. Tragically, about 2000 bears meet this end throughout the US and Canada each year.

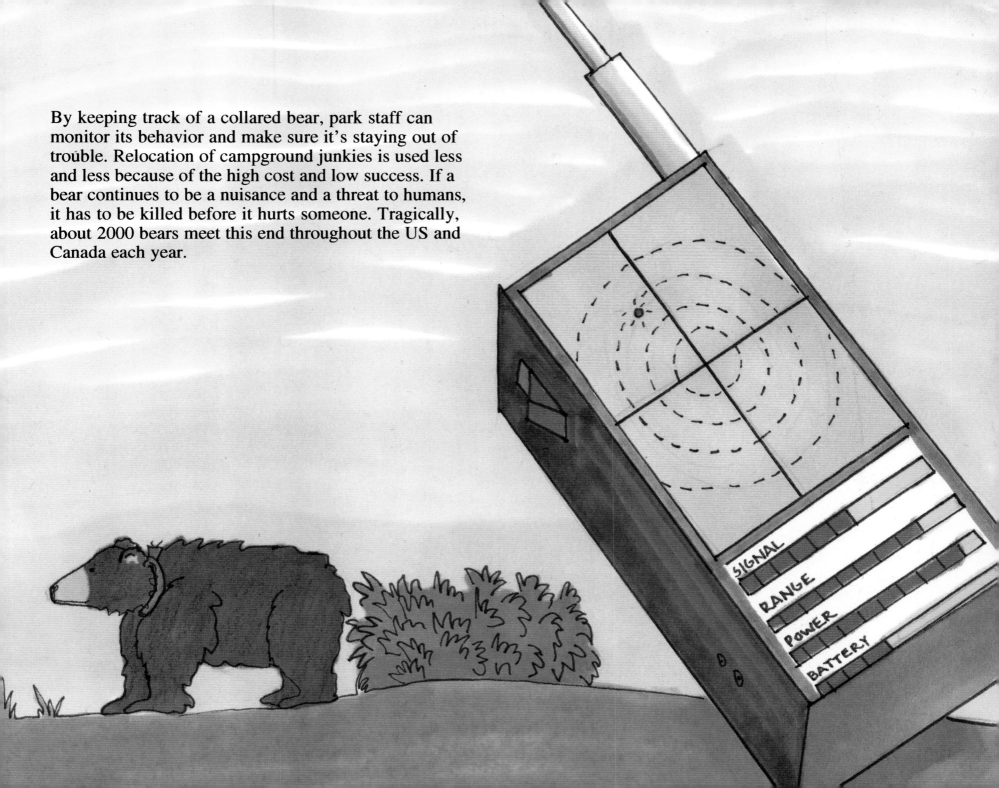

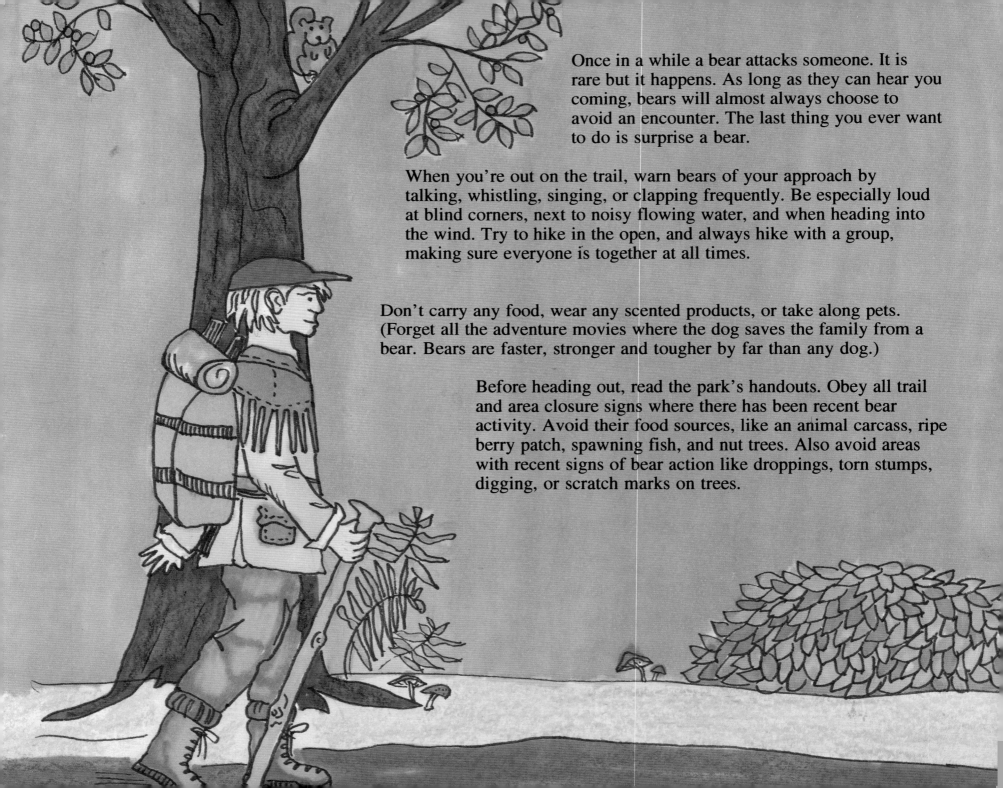

Once in a while a bear attacks someone. It is rare but it happens. As long as they can hear you coming, bears will almost always choose to avoid an encounter. The last thing you ever want to do is surprise a bear.

When you're out on the trail, warn bears of your approach by talking, whistling, singing, or clapping frequently. Be especially loud at blind corners, next to noisy flowing water, and when heading into the wind. Try to hike in the open, and always hike with a group, making sure everyone is together at all times.

Don't carry any food, wear any scented products, or take along pets. (Forget all the adventure movies where the dog saves the family from a bear. Bears are faster, stronger and tougher by far than any dog.)

Before heading out, read the park's handouts. Obey all trail and area closure signs where there has been recent bear activity. Avoid their food sources, like an animal carcass, ripe berry patch, spawning fish, and nut trees. Also avoid areas with recent signs of bear action like droppings, torn stumps, digging, or scratch marks on trees.

If you and a bear do find each other, don't run or
yell. A bear is more likely to chase a person
running away. Let the bear know you are not
threatening or challenging it. Speak calmly as you
back away slowly. Don't show your teeth and
don't face the bear head-on.

Bears rise up on two feet when they are trying to
get a better look or sniff at something. If bears
feel threatened they may bluff a charge on all
fours and veer away at the last moment. Rarely,
but occasionally, a bear really means it and
follows through with the charge.

Experts generally advise to play dead if a
grizzly charges and fight back if a black
bear charges. You must remember there
are no guarantees with bears. Each one is
an individual with its own way of
responding.

Sometimes there is less food than usual for bears because of weather and other changing conditions. When this happens, bears may come searching for food in the peopled areas of the park. These are not social visits, and it's very important that the bears don't find anything but their natural food sources. Not only does our food make bears dangerous and unhealthy, it also ruins the natural way they control their own population in areas that can not support more bears.

A female bear that has mated in spring carries the fertilized egg all through summer and fall, but it doesn't develop unless the bear's body gives the go-ahead signal. If the bear has had plenty to eat and has enough body fat, the egg will begin growing in the fall. However, if it has been a lean year without a good food supply, the egg will not develop and the bear's body will wait until the area can support more bears, before producing cubs. This beautiful balance is ruined if the bear finds garbage or people food. Bears can live more than 20 or 25 years, but most of the bears in the wild are less than ten years old.

This bear shouldn't have cubs this year. Her territory has recently been logged and can't support more bears at this time.

These bear sisters' territory is lush with natural food sources for pregnant bears and their cubs.

The blind, bald helpless cubs are born
in January, weighing about as
little as rats. They don't
open their eyes for six
weeks.

In late fall,
after eating
as much as
possible, the
bears curl up
in their dens to
sleep while food is
not available. The layer of fat
a bear stores up provides enough energy
and insulation to sustain it through the winter.

While mom sleeps, they crawl blindly over her, snuggling up and drinking her milk till she wakes up in spring. While they grow very fast and get stronger, she loses 20-40% of her own weight.

The bears emerge from the den in spring. The cubs will face many dangers and only about half of them will live to age three. However, more and more people are learning to value and protect wild animals, assuring their place and survival in our modern world. Humans are even smarter than the average bear and we are making great strides in the research, management and protection of bears.

Parks, reserves and wilderness areas are special homes for bears. All these places are made richer for having bears, and we are the lucky visitors. The bears' survival as magnificent wild animals depends on our respect and intelligent use of our shared land. When you see a healthy bear living naturally as a wild creature, you have proof that we can save what is left on our earth by working together.

Meanwhile, your teddy is safe and sound at home waiting for a hug and a picnic. Let him remind you of the very different big beautiful wild bears out there right now looking for food, water and shelter the way they always have.